HYENA

RHINOCEROS

KOALA

OSTRICH

Owl

PIRANHA

Chameleon

TOUCAN

CAMEL

OTTER

WOLF

MEERCHAT

PORCUPINE

WARTHOG

FLAMINGO

SNAKE

HIPPOPOTAMUS

ZEBRA

DEER

EMU'

Fox

BEAR

GIRAFFE

KANGAROO

GORILLA

PANTHER

MACAQUE MONKEY

WILDCAT

ALLIGATOR

TIGER

CHEETAH

LION

LIONESS

LEOPARD

GAZELLE

EAGLE

BUFFALO

MONKEY

HIPPOPOTAMUS

CHIMPANCES

www.ingramcontent.com/pod-product-compliance
Lightning Source LLC
Chambersburg PA
CBHW080506030726
47592CB00011B/3270